Dwight Damon Presents

The Amazing Stone-Deaf Hypnotist

Dr. Rexford L. North

ISBN # 1-885846-09-6

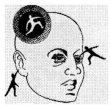 Advanced Studies Consultants

The Beginning

Table of Contents

First Issue of the
Journal of Hypnotism
May 1951
8½ × 5½ – 24 pages

Journal of Hypnotism™
March 2006
8½ × 11½ – 84 pages

DR. REXFORD L. NORTH

DR. REXFORD L. NORTH MEMORIAL TROPHY

Top Award Presented
Annually at the
National Guild of Hypnotists'
Convention

Dr. Rexford L. North and
The Boston Hypnotism Center
The Years 1949–1956

A small number of us continue to research all the available bits and pieces of information about Dr. Rexford L. North, a most extraordinary man who overcame the so-called "handicap" of total deafness to become one of the most outstanding stage and club hypnotists of his time—a man who was a living example of the power of positive thinking as he parlayed his last eighteen dollars into a publishing business and teaching facility that was truly unique. This has been an ongoing quest for the past fifty years. Now we would like to share the facts with you.

Memories of Dr. Rexford L. North

After losing his hearing due to spinal meningitis, reportedly contracted while on a U.S.O. tour, Rex North, once a popular hypnotist on the vaudeville and night-club circuits, was to all accounts, down and out. Without his hearing he felt that he could no longer amaze audiences with his hypnotism and mentalism presentations—it just wasn't meant for him to return to the show business life he loved. Yet, bit by bit, with the encouragement of friends he tried to adapt to a world of silence. Small club dates for friendly audiences in the area of Cliffside Park, NJ helped him to regain some of the important confidence needed to succeed as an entertainer, and unusual publicity stunts helped him to reestablish his skills as a performer on a local basis around the Palisades Park area.

One such stunt was arranged when North read that extreme change in pressures could possibly restore hearing in some cases of complete deafness. He arranged for a newspaper to publicize an attempt to do this with a DC3 twin-prop plane. The plane would take off and fly up to a specified altitude high over the countryside where the pilot would then go into a power dive before pulling up at a safe level. This would result in a drastic change in pressure for all aboard, and might possibly cause a reversal of his hearing loss. A number of local residents who also had extreme hearing loss also volunteered to participate in the stunt. Although not successful in the restoration of his hearing the event received widespread publicity for the hypnotist and resulted in more theatrical bookings, which eventually brought him to back to the attention of theatrical agents who had more or less written him off after his hearing loss.

While in the Providence, Rhode Island area he signed for a summer-long booking at a small resort on nearby Block Island. (image at left) This seven-night-a-week engagement gave him the confidence that he needed to eventually regain his status as a crowd-pleasing theatrical hypnotist, but didn't exactly prove to be a lucrative booking after all the expenses were handled. With little money in his wallet he moved with his tuxedo, extensive press books of past exploits, and a portable Underwood typewriter to Boston, Massachusetts. He secured a reasonably priced room at the Broadway, a theatrical hotel, home to professional wrestler's, night club jugglers and other traveling entertainers. He also reserved a small meeting room for one night each week the following four weeks at the popular Hotel Bradford in the theater district. More money was spent on flyers advertising his free lecture demonstration at the Bradford and window cards with an invitation to *Learn Genuine Hypnotism*. He personally distributed and placed the flyers and window cards throughout downtown Boston and the die was cast. He checked his wallet and there was eighteen dollars remaining in his entire bankroll.

People who attended the free lecture-demonstrations were truly mesmerized by this mysterious looking man with the strange voice and without fail there were.enrollees who, before they left, paid the advance registration for a future class.

Every day, North scoured the city on foot and by subway for a suitable location for what would be the Hypnotism Center of Boston where he would hold that first class. Quite by chance he came across a Spiritualist conference, open to the public, at Huntington Chambers. While in the building lobby he noticed that there was an office vacancy available in that prestigious 30 Huntington

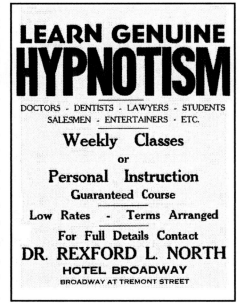

Avenue building. He inquired and found that the previous tenants had left a collection of office furniture which would be included if the next tenant was interested. A rental agreement was signed using part of the class deposits and Dr. Rexford L. North now had a physical location where small classes could be conducted.

In the interest of economizing he decided to sleep on a sofa which came with the furnishings in the new office. He continued the free lecture-demonstrations at the Hotel Bradford since they were attracting attendees each week and the next class was lining up. After ten weeks the first Boston class graduated in the fall of 1949. Young members of that class who became charter members of the National Guild of Hypnotists in 1950-51, and later were Advisory Board members during its re-organization include Frank Anderson, Berchman Carville and Dwight Damon.

1st Boston class graduation 1949—Emerson College student Dwight Damon receives "cum laude" congratulations from Dr. Rexford L. North. Deceased NGH charter and board members Berchman Carville and Frank Anderson are directly behind the congratulatory handshake.

Within a couple of weeks, as enrollment for the second class grew, it was obvious that more space was needed. Just by chance, a suite which included a private office and a large room suitable for lectures and classes became available on another floor. The building manager said the previous tenant had also left a lot of chairs in the large room, which he had no use for, and they were also included. The free lecture demonstrations could now be moved to the same location as the office and classroom.

Within a year it was evident that an even larger facility was needed for classes and lectures as well as publishing and mail-order. A location was found at 26 Saint Botolph Street, a rather Bohemian street of stately Brownstones, whose occupants were artists, writers, poets, and also the home of the prestigious Vesper George Art School.

Dr John C. Hughes' first impression when attending one of the Monday night lecture-demonstrations follows—

"Little did I realize when I set out one cold night in the winter of 1951 to attend a lecture in Boston that I was doing something which would change the whole course of my life. I still remember with vivid pleasure how I felt when I walked through the doors of the Hypnotism Center for the first time. I remember my first impression of Dr. Rexford L North. He was the very image of a hypnotist—the figure who stepped upon the platform had a dignified professional bearing, long, black hair, piercing, tiny Lilliputian eyes behind glasses, and a trim Vandyke beard. North was stone deaf and the inflection of his voice had an eerie quality about it; he nevertheless managed to modulate his voice well enough so it did not clash with the rest of the image he projected.

Charismatic is the impression he made, and we listened spellbound while he enlightened us about '... that strange, mysterious power which charms and fascinates men and women, influences their thoughts, controls their desires, and has the power to make you the supreme master of every situation.' At the conclusion of his fascinating lecture and demonstration we knew that life was full of alluring possibilities if we signed up for his course in 'genuine hypnotism' and mastered the secrets of hypnotic influence. It is no wonder that he was idolized by the students who came to his Hypnotism Center. Those of us who are still alive and active in hypnosis today remember Dr. North with keen affection."

The move to 26 Saint Botolph from 30 Huntington was only a matter of blocks and was accomplished with the help of graduates and their stations wagons. John Conroy knew where to borrow a floor sander, Dwight Damon knew how to operate it, and an attractive hardwood floor was revealed under the previous tenant's gray paint in the large lecture hall. A small stage was constructed, with a huge hypnodisk for a backdrop and now the lecture demonstrations, classes and so forth had seating for about 40–50 people.

Now, the Boston Hypnotism Center truly had an impressive location which offered a very large lecture hall, two private offices for client work, rooms for publication preparation and on the lower level, a complete apartment which opened to a communal courtyard. Neighboring tenants who abutted the courtyard were truly Bohemian in nature—a poet, photographer, writer, artists and, last but not least, an attractive dancer, her lover, and her seven foot tall husband who came out only after dark.

The constant promotion to attract prospective students to study in the classes was stepped up with 50 cent discount passes (off the new $1.50 admission) being circulated

widely throughout Boston. Word of mouth and getting the discount passes out resulted in larger crowds for the lecture-demonstrations. The lecture nights always brought a large number of new prospects for the hypnotism classes as well as a number of graduates who liked being with the group and who became the nucleus for the first hypnotism organization of it's kind.

It was decided to add weekly lecture-demonstrations and classes at New York City's prestigious Carnegie Hall suites, but the weekly train commute and overhead, and without the promotion efforts that had been accomplished in Boston, it just wasn't worthwhile to continue after about a month. Boston was truly the home of the Hypnotism Center and with two demos a week, a couple of classes and preparation of materials, there wasn't time to expand to New York City.

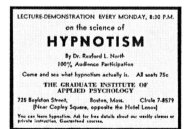

However, a plan to publish a magazine for hypnotists and hypnologists was brewing in Dr. North's mind. Harry Arons was a friendly competitor, who owned Power Publishers in New Jersey. Arons and North often collaborated on products for the mail order end of both entities, so his opinion was solicited. He agreed to loan us his list of mail order clients, but cautioned that "It's going to be a waste of postage stamps" yet, he offered to write for the new magazine and was listed as a Contributing Editor along with Bernie Yanover. Dwight Damon who was a regular employee of the Hypnotism Center was also an editor, handling re-write, layout, collating, mailing, duplication and anything else that needed to be done on folios plus the new magazine. Contributing columnists were Maurice Kershaw, Ormond McGill, Herbert Charles, Melvin Powers, Raphael H.Rhodes and others.

The *Journal of Hypnotism* was launched using our mailing lists and those of Harry Arons to get started. The magazine was about the size of a *Readers Digest*, but a lot thinner since it only ran twenty pages. The magazine caught on and ran until 1956, much to Harry Aron's dismay. In 1956 converted to a tabloid newspaper format and published as *Hypnotism* for one issue.

With the revitalization of the Guild in 1986 the *New Journal of Hypnotism* resumed publication, changing back to the *Journal of Hypnotism* in 1988 and with up to 80 pages, a full color cover and many outstanding columnists is currently published quarterly. A companion publication, the *Hypno-Gram* is also published for Guild members between *Journals*.

Mail often arrived at Boston's main Post Office in the late 40s–early 50s, addressed only to "Hypnotist, Boston, Mass", or even with a caricature-like sketch of the a man with a moustache, Van Dyke beard and hyp-  notic-looking eyes. Generally these cryptic letters found their way to the Back Bay Annex and the intended recipient, Dr. Rexford L. North.

The above photo shows Jini Shea, Boston model, in a deep trance, having been hypnotized over the phone by Dr. Rexford L. North. Tom Riley, feature reporter on the Boston American, is shown pinching her right arm which has been made completely anesthetic through Dr. North's suggestion. Miss Shea and Mr. Riley were photographed in the offices of the Boston American while Dr. North was several miles away at the other end of the phone in his office at 30 Huntington Avenue. The experiment was especially remarkable because Dr. North is totally deaf and could not hear what was going on at the newspaper office He talked over the phone to induce the trance and gave Miss Shea all suggestions for experiments in anesthesia, amnesia and a positive hallucination while someone else had to give him written notes to keep him informed on what was going on and what was being said over the phone from the newspaper office.

In a no time at all he had definitely become a well-known Boston celebrity of sorts and was in demand for shows and classes. In those years television was in its infancy and he was often being contacted for TV appearances, and was a regular guest on radio shows which originating from local night spots. Although the Boston newspapers still didn't accept ads for hypnotism classes he nevertheless received many interesting interviews by newspaper columnists such as the *Record American's* Tom Riley.

Yes, this man had come to Boston and taken it by storm with his ability to attract publicity. One of the largest cities in the world had come to know him well enough that his mail was delivered without name and address, but only a sketch on the envelope. Yet, with all this free publicity he found that Boston newspapers would not accept paid advertising for hypnotism classes. This was true throughout puritanical New England for many years.

There is no denying that Rexford L. North created a world of mystery and speculation, not only because he was the consummate hypnotist in an era that still thought of the practitioner of the art as possessing some strange powers over others, ala Svengali, but also because he made every effort to play upon those almost superstitious false ideas that the general public had. Yes, he was a showman par excellence and he knew the value of publicity in building his reputation; yet he also had a perverse sense of humor which compelled him to do many outrageous and unconventional things, which only added fuel to the fire for those who beheld him with a jaundiced eye.

Yet aside from the unconventional world of publicity, there was still another Dr. Rexford L. North—a man devoted to the world of hypnotism. The Hypnotism Center of Boston, Massachusetts, became the Mecca for hypnotists from all over the globe, as well as many curious local citizens who attended the weekly lecture-demonstrations and classes.

There was no such thing as an eight-hour workday or five-day-work week at this fountainhead of hypnotism. We constantly worked to reach more and more people with our courses, lecture-demonstrations, books and publications. When the boss worked around the clock, he expected his assistant, college-student Dwight Damon, to do the same. It was fortunate indeed that that there were also many enthusiastic volunteer helpers dropping by the Center seven days a week.

There were always new ideas and projects to work on such as the weekly class at Carnegie Hall in New York City. At the same time we planned and produced a first in the field—recording the ten-lesson hypnotism course for home-study—another first in the field of hypnotism.

The charisma of the man inspired people from all walks of life to participate in many ways, and though they never expected compensation, he had a way of letting them know they were appreciated for their help and support. This guru of the power of suggestion found a devoted coterie of disciples in his endeavors.

The regulars at the Hypnotism Center never had the opportunity to pay for a meal at the nearby Waldorf or Hayes Bickford cafeterias when we took a late-night break. On after-meeting jaunts to Chinatown many an unknowing first-timer would find himself "outdrawn" for the check by our hypnotism guru. This was not an ego-building ploy, but rather just another display of the quiet generosity of a really fine person. And, at the Hypnotism Center when anyone arrived or left, there was always a genuinely sincere handshake from Dr. North.

Rexford L. North was by all odds the premier hypnotist of the late 1940s and early 1950s, as a showman, a teacher and a therapist. He was foremost in getting dental hypnosis accepted by the medical and dental authorities of the Boston area, through a series of practical demonstrations of its effectiveness in 1949-50.

Many students of the Hypnotism Center have gone on to careers in the profession. One of North's students, who would become an important figure in the field of hypnotism. Martin T. Orne established an influential research center—the Studies in Hypnosis Project at the Massachusetts Mental Health Center under the auspices of Harvard University. The research center was later transferred to the University of Pennsylvania under the name of the Unit for Experimental Psychiatry. Orne was then a professor of psychiatry and in full charge of the program, along with his wife, Emily, who had been associated with the laboratory from the beginning. In 1962, Orne took over as editor of the *International Society for Clinical and Experimental Hypnosis Journal*. The most outstanding among Orne's many contributions to the theory and practice of hypnotherapy has been the clear distinction he drew between the essence of hypnotism—that is, the phenomenon of suggestibility by itself—and the artifacts, or the physical effects produced by hypnosis. Even among the most careful investigators of hypnotic phenomena there had always been some uncertainty about the relationship between the act of suggestion and its results. After Orne, there could no longer be any such intermingling of cause and effect, and this resulted in greater clarity in the definition and application of hypnosis.

And there were others who made their marks, but let's take a brief look at how Dr. North's brainchild, the National Guild of Hypnotists achieved the preeminence that Dr. North envisioned.

Dr. North was the man who had the idea for an organization of this type, as well as the founding of the *Journal of Hypnotism*. He was a friend and mentor to Dwight Damon, John Hughes, Maurice Kershaw, Ormond McGill, Arnold Levison and others who are still very active in the Guild and the profession.

Once again North consulted with Harry Arons. This time with his idea of starting a national organization for hypnotists. Word was that Harry had been unhappy that his previous prediction about "wasting the cost of stamps" to start the *Journal* had been wrong and now he said an organization of hypnotists was a foolish idea.

Late in 1950 and early '51, with a handful of students at the Hypnotism Center in Boston, Dr. North organized the National Guild of Hypnotists. George Rogers was president, and Arnold Levison treasurer. One of the pictures in our archives shows Dr. North presenting Harry Arons with his membership certificate during Harry's visit to the Boston Hypnotism Center.

Thirty-five years later when the Guild literature named some of its distinguished past and present members, Dr. Dwight Damon received a call from Harry Arons who asked that his name not be used because he had never been a member. When told about the picture, he said that unless the Guild could produce a membership application signed by him he would never admit being a member. Of course, in the early days of the Guild you just paid your $5 dues and after your name was entered on the rolls you received a certificate and membership card. Subscriptions to the *Journal of Hypnotism* were separate. Coincidently, when the National Guild of Hypnotists started to grow Harry Arons started the Association for the Advancement of Ethical Hypnosis (AAEH) which operated very successfully under his direction for many years and included a magazine for its members. Although approached several times by the Guild president/editor, Dr. Damon, Arons would not agree to being interviewed for the *Journal of Hypnotism* until his last days and then it was too late and so he was honored in the publication posthumously in December of 1997.

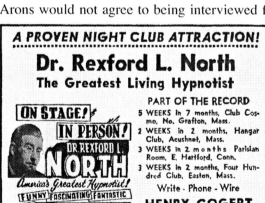

In the 1950s a number of NGH chapters had been established across the country and in Canada. In those early years the *Journal of Hypnotism* became the bond that tied it all together and still reaches hypnotists around the world. People joined NGH, received a membership card, subscribed to the *Journal of Hypnotism* and that was about it, unless they lived in a city that had chapter meetings. There were half a dozen chapters established across the U.S. which eventually grew to over seventy-five in fifty-five countries.

At that time 90 to 95 percent of the membership consisted of stage hypnotists and hobbyists. About 5 to 10 percent could actually be classified as hypnotherapists; they were the licensed health professionals, such as psychologists, physicians, etc.

Being a close-knit organization allowed a lot of cliques to be formed and power struggles to emerge, and eventually the overall substance of the organization dwindled as other groups spun off and developed by operating in a more autocratic manner. Yet a small band of founding members kept in touch and worked together in various ways through the years to keep the Guild alive. Several of these members held the dream of re-organizing some day to make the Guild a truly meaningful organization.

Two of the founding members, Dwight F. Damon and John C. Hughes, were attending the same college and conducted courses using the course originally developed for the Hypnotism Center by Dr. Rexford L. North. After graduation both men returned to New England to establish private practices as doctors of chiropractic.

An opportunity to re-build the Guild was discussed and Dr. Damon took the helm as President/Executive Director. Dr. Hughes became Research Editor of the *Journal of Hypnotism* which was re-born as the *New Journal of Hypnotism*. Another founding member, Frank Anderson, started manufacturing electronic devices for use by practicing hypnotists and the marketing resources of Elsom Eldridge's Achievement Center were made available to help revitalize The National Guild of Hypnotists which was incorporated as a not-for-profit organization with headquarters in Merrimack, New Hampshire.

From those humble beginnings few other than North himself could have foreseen that five decades later thousands of active hypnotists the world over would claim membership in the Guild. Indeed the name National Guild of Hypnotists is now a misnomer, it is truly an international organization in over 65 countries.

There are those who would point out that Dr. Rexford. L. North had a reputation quite the opposite of what we are relating and would attribute our character appraisal to adulation and naivete by his protegeés. But that is not the case, because if anyone was aware of the character weaknesses of this man, it would have to be Dwight Damon. Working and living at the Hypnotism Center, he came to know the flaws, fears, indulgences and indiscriminations more than anyone, but he and his family also came to know another side of this fascinating man who was, in his own way, a genius.

In 1955 a final move was made to 725 Boylston Street and the facility also became the headquarters for the Graduate Institute of Applied Psychology. Located high in the front of the building the large windows overlooked the impressive headquarters and Mother-church of the Christian Scientists. Dr. North would stand at the window overlooking the Christian Science complex, and smiling say, "If only Mary Baker Eddy could see us now!"

In the fall of 1956 rumors started to circulate from Boston to hypnotists across the country—North had disappeared without a trace. There was no activity at the office on Boylston Street . . . his last correspondence indicated he was going to Maine to present a show for a service club ... someone thought he had died in an auto accident . . . another that he was murdered on the streets of Chicago . . . and even that his hearing had returned and after all those years of silence it was too much to handle, so he had a mental breakdown or became a member of a silent monastery . . . take your choice.

Whatever the case may be, his memory is honored at the NGH conventions. A number of honors and awards are given at the annual conventions, with the recipients chosen by their peers. Most prestigious of these awards is the coveted Dr. Rexford L. North Memorial Trophy given in honor of the Guild's founder which is awarded by his protege, Dr. Dwight F. Damon, Guild president.

In the words of Dr. John C. Hughes, "Dr. Rexford L. North is remembered as well for what he accomplished in bringing hypnosis and its practical applications to the attention of the general public and of the medical profession. In a very large sense, to those who had the privilege of knowing him, the contemporary history of hypnotism could be dated B.N. and A.N.—i.e., Before North and After North. One generation plants the trees; another sits in their shade. Here's to you, Dr. Rexford L. North, for planting those trees."

Regarding the contents of this book:

In the late 1940s and early 1950s, outside the mainstream psychology world, most of the so-called books that were published about hypnotism would be considered folios or booklets and would often be mimeographed, since photocopying wasn't yet on the scene. In our HypnoClassics™ series we have brought many of these long out of print booklets together in compilations for those in the 21st century who are students of the art and science of hypnotism—the avid hypnologist.

Our publications, *The Best of Harry Arons*, *The Master Course in Hypnotism*, *Power Hypnosis*, and *Dr. Rexford L. North and the Boston Hypnotism Center* present information from the past that is still applicable to present-day hypnotism practices. Now we are bringing these classics as they were originally written to you in a reasonably-priced, contemporary format. Whether you purchase these books for their historical value in your library or with the hope of learning something new, we thank you for your interest in what is an important part of the development of hypnotism in America after WWII.

The HypnoClassic™ series has been created to highlight the many individual contributions made by hypnotists half a century ago to the art and science of hypnotism. No claims of accuracy or efficacy of techniques or theories presented in that era are made by the publisher. However, there are many techniques currently in use which are hundreds or even thousands of years old.

Remember that the art and science of hypnotism is an exciting new profession that is actually thousands of years old. It has often been said that the first use of suggestion (hypnotism) is reported to appear in Genesis 2:21 in the Bible.

The Boston Hypnotism Center
Photos & Profiles
1950–1956

Arnold Levison
1st Treasurer

George Rogers
1st President

Dr. Rexford L. North
Founder

Dr. Rexford L. North and Harry Arons

HYPNOTISM

Guaranteed 10,000 Circulation

15¢ per Copy

With which is combined the "HYPNOTIC EDUCATIONAL BULLETIN" and "THE JOURNAL OF HYPNOTISM"

Vol. 14, No. 11 — NOVEMBER, 1956 — $1.50 per year

Hypnotism In The News

(Editor's note: At the present time there is a greater interest in hypnotism than ever before. Newspapers and magazines are giving more space to the subject. We know that many readers of HYPNOTISM MONTHLY are interested in these articles and therefore, each month we will list all current publications having such stories. We ask the co-operation of readers in sending us clippings of any articles and stories they come across. When sending clippings, please be sure to include the date of issue and the name of the publication. Send all items to: NEWS EDITOR, HYPNOTISM MONTHLY, 725 Boylston Street, Boston 16, Mass.)

Scotland Yard and Hypnotism

The Miami Herald of August 31, 1956, tells of an investigation being conducted by Scotland Yard at Eastborne, England, into the deaths of some 300 widows who passed on between 1934 and 1953.

Healing Through Hypnotism

Hypnotism cannot cure any human ailment— any more than any doctor, any medicine, any treatment or any therapy can cure any human ailment. Yet there are many cases of human abnormalities where, without the use of hypnotism, the most advanced medical remedies and treatments are powerless. The truth is, as any thinking human being will verify: no medicine, no treatment, no remedy has CURED any DISEASE. Only Mother Nature cures and medicines and treatments are administered by practitioners merely to AID and HASTEN Nature's work. Hypnotism, which, without drugs or other medical or surgical aids, completely relaxes the ailing human being, permits Nature to do her healing uninipeded and in the shortest, possible time. Records show conclusively that through the use of hypnotism many sick and ailing persons regain health — sometimes with miraculous speed. This journal carries the latest advices, covering the progress of hypnotism as an adjunct to medicine, treatments and surgery used by leading scientists throughout the world. Perhaps you, my faithful reader, will find in these or later columns the positive answers to your most perplexing health problems.

Dr. Rexford L. North

Dental Hypnosis: A Case History

By John C. Hughes

Therapeutic application of hypnosis in dentistry is relatively an...

Hypnotism & Chiropractic

By DR. HERBERT CHARLES

Chiropractors, as a general rule, are practitioners who are quick to take advantage of new modes and methods in the art of natural healing and hypnosis has had its full share of "going over" by these doctors who are convinced that most human ailments originate in some displacement of the bones of the spine.

One of the most difficult problems confronting the chiropractor has been tenseness on the part of the sufferer and the inability to utilize the full benefits of chiropractic in certain cases because of this inability of the patient to relax.

I might also say that the great stumbling block to more widespread and successful application of hypnotism in chiropractic has been the lack of the precise methodology to be employed. The folio, of which this article is a condensation, seeks to solve that problem. The chiropractor has looked with interest at hypnotism and has been quick to recognize the possibility of its usage in chiropractic. Busily engaged in his daily practice, he has been unable to extract from the general knowledge of the available literature a procedure suitable for his needs. The tools are there but no specific instruction as to how they should be used in his particular field.

The science of chiropractic like that of hypnotism has been beset since its inception by charges of ... and quackery. Like hyp-time patients of chiropractors are people who have already visited medical doctors without satisfaction or cure of their symptoms. When the chiropractor is successful in his treatment the patient becomes an unpaid advertiser. He may even over-emphasize the benefits gained, because due to the unfortunate antagonism of the medical profession a stigma is attached to the chiropractic and the patient feels a necessity to praise the chiropractor in order to justify his going to him. When the chiropractor employs hypnotism a certain transference takes place that makes of the patient a militant advocate of chiropractic. Instead of an apologist and such is his own your hehalf in convincing most of his hearers. This attitude is not mentioned merely...

1956 tabloid newspaper *HYPNOTISM* succeeded
the original *JOURNAL OF HYPNOTISM of the 50s*

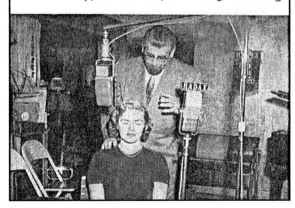

Dr. North Hypnotizes Subject During Recording

INTERNATIONAL HYPNOLOGICAL ASSOCIATION

26 Saint Botolph Street · Boston 16, Massachusetts

This Is To Certify That

John Hughes

Is a member in good standing to the date below

Professional Membership No. — Valid to — Signed by

102 — Lifetime — *R. Standish*

TREASURER

Membership card of our
affiliate organization,
The International
Hypnological Association

Pictured above (left to right): Dr. Rexford L. North, Charles Nichols, George Rogers, NGH Chairman and Sol Bernstein

Fall 1950

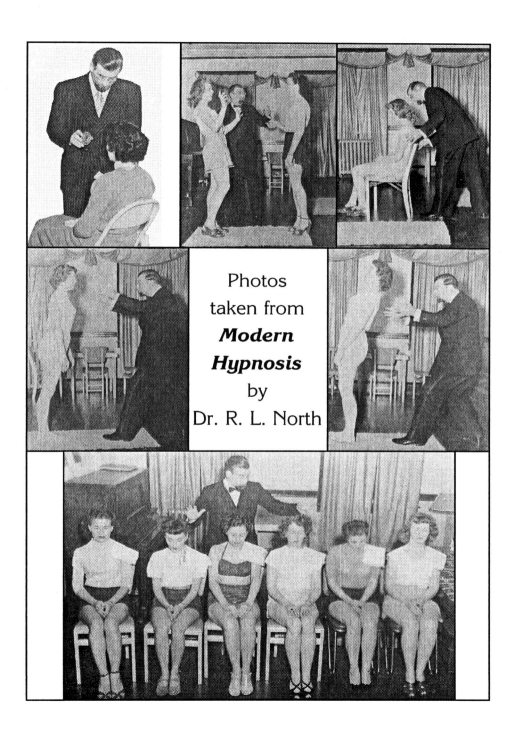

Photos taken from
Modern Hypnosis
by
Dr. R. L. North

Dr. North re: "Pulp" Magazine Ads

EDITORIAL

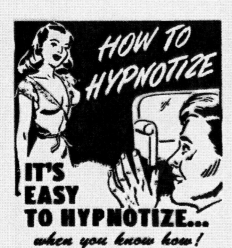

■ In the last issue we started a policy of exposing the abuses to which hypnotism is subjected. This issue we call your attention to an ad that appears in many of the cheaper magazines every month.

The text states, "Want the thrill of imposing your will over someone? Of making someone do exactly as you order? Try hypnotism!" This is aptly illustrated with a male (presumably a purchaser of the book) getting ready to "impose his will" on a sexy looking female. There is a convenient couch in the background. The implication is all too obvious. Anybody old enough to read the ad will get the idea that the advertiser is trying to put over. Added bait is the inclusion of "24 revealing photographs with the text. This is a rather cute offer. First of all the photographs are not what the prospective buyer expects. Not only are the pictures quite proper — but the course itself deals with rhythmic breathing. The text is by Konradi Leitner, and is called the Master Key to Hypnotism. While rhythmic breathing might be a good idea for wolves to practice, it certainly won't help their projects.

Why are we opposed to this type of promotion? First of all the man who is lured into buying will be defrauded, and he will be justified in rejecting the real value of HYPNOTISM. What is far more important is, the overwhelming majority of people who read the ad, but don't buy the book, will certainly get a very wrong idea of hypnotism. Fortunately what such ads suggest, cannot be done. The general public should not be exposed to this type of trash. It is these beliefs, fostered by this misinformation that have prevented hypnotism from reaching the level of achievement it deserves.

REXFORD L. NORTH

Journal of Hypnotism Vol. 2 No. 4, January, 1953

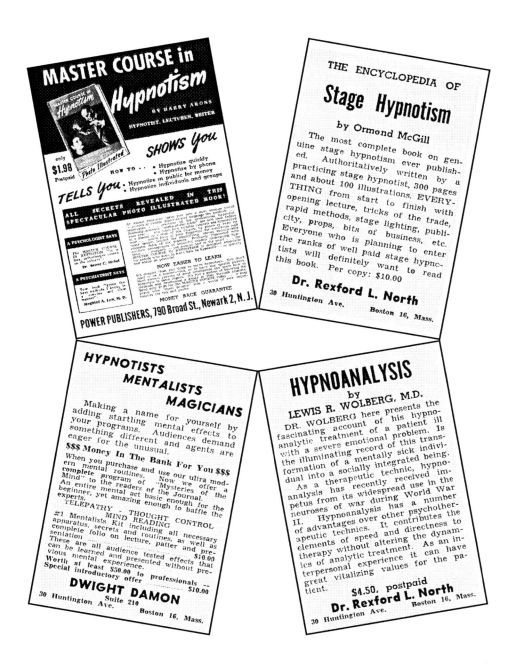

HYPNOTISM ADVERTISING EVOLVES IN THE 50S

DR. DWIGHT F. DAMON, FNGH
PRESIDENT OF NGH

Dwight F. Damon, D.C. FNGH is Editor of *The Journal of Hypnotism*™ and the *Hypno-Gram*™, President of NFH 104 OPEIU-AFL/CIO and a founding member of NGH.

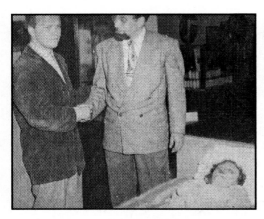

Hypnotic "Window Sleep"
Beautyrest Sponsorship Promoting
Stage Show Appearances—1950

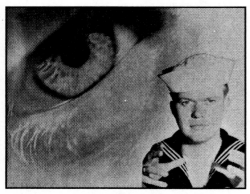

Performing in USO and Service Club
Shows 1951–1954

HILARIOUS HYPNOSIS

IN PERSON

DAMON

ON STAGE

TONITE ONLY

1950s Stage Shows on ATC Circuit

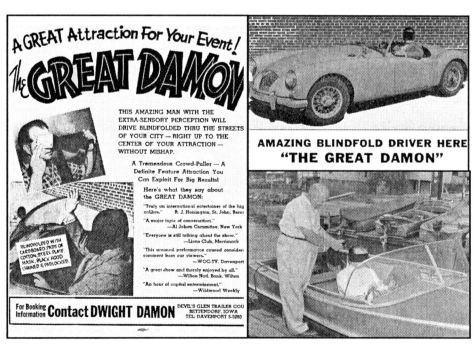

Midwestern shows from WOC-TV - Davenport, Iowa

Dr. John C. Hughes, DNGH

John C. Hughes, DC, DNGH, is Research Editor of the *Journal of Hypnotism*. NGH Board Certified Diplomate. The founder of the Philippine Hypnodontic Society and founding member of NGH.

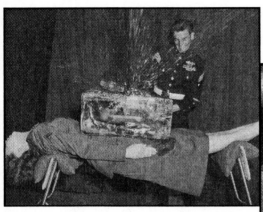

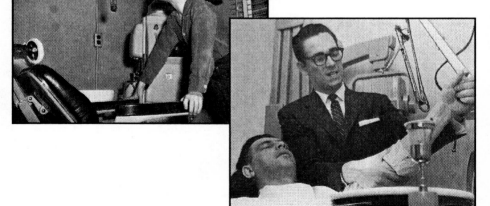

John Hughes International Tour

Berchman Carville has just returned on 30 days leave from the Korean war and told us of many interesting experiences. The one that I liked best was the time he was injured by a hand grenade. Upon arrival at the aid station the doctor told him they were running low on chemical anesthetics and asked if he thought he could stand the pain while having the shrapnel removed. Carville explained that he was able to use auto-suggestion to make himself anesthetic and then did it. The doctor was amazed.

Dr. North has been doing quite a few dates lately for Lions, Rotary and Kiwanis clubs.

Journal of Hypnotism
Vol. 1 No. 3 • Sept. 1951

MAURICE KERSHAW, FNGH

Maurice Kershaw, B.S., FNGH is Chairman of the NGH
Certification Board and a founding member of NGH

Early years in Canada
appearing in Night Clubs
& other venues—1950s

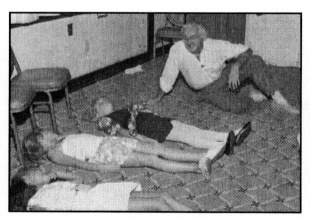

Pediatric Hypnosis

Presenting at the
NGH Convention

ARNOLD LEVISON, PH.D.

Arnold Levison, Ph.D., was a founding member and first treasurer of NGH. He currently serves as historian and curator of the historical exhibit at the annual convention.

A young Levison as first
Treasurer of the NGH

2005 NGH Convention
Historical Exhibit

THE 1ST HYPNO-GRAM™
PUBLISHED MARCH 1997

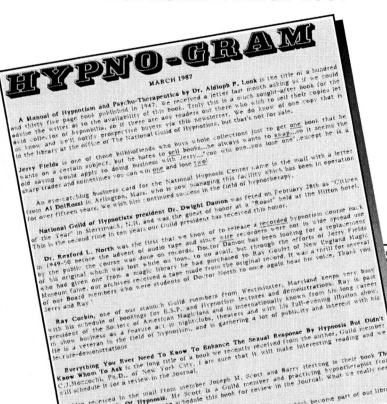

8 ½ × 6
Two-sided
Newsletter

...... Guild of Hypnotists member survey sheets are important to you and to the organization, so please fill out and return yours immediately to help us compile the facts and figures. This information will help us to provide articles, monographs, books, tapes, publications and seminars that will be of the greatest benefit for the most members. Every member counts and although we know that it is a fact of life that a few members won't fill out the forms and return them, we still look for a large return. Survey sheets are scheduled to be enclosed in the March issue of the Journal or the Hypno-Gram......watch for yours.

VERY IMPORTANT - With every mailing we receive a number of returns from the Post Office of mail that is unforwardable because a member moved and did not fill out proper Post Office forwarding forms or the forwarding period has run out. Don't let this happen to you. If you move let us know directly and we will put the change into our computer so that you will not miss even one issue of the Journal or Hypno-Gram or notices of continuing-education seminars. You are important to us, so don't fall by the wayside.

Steven LaVelle Seminars schdedule is included in this issue of the Hypno-Gram, so please check the dates whether you are interested in monitoring as a refresher or attending for the first time to become a certified hypnotherapist. We are making every effort this year to plan and announce all seminar dates well in advance so interested members can arrange to attend, but it is important to register early since both the Guild and the Hypnodyne Foundation are booking medium capacity function rooms. We mutually feel that their is more individual benefits received when classes are kept to an easily managed size.

THE CURRENT HYPNO-GRAM™
PUBLISHED JAN/FEB 2006

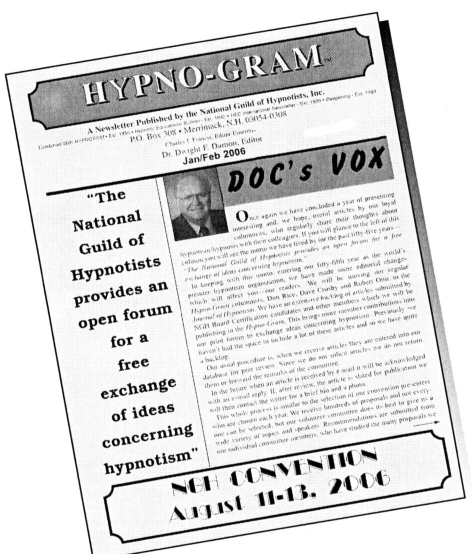

8 ½ × 11 – 24 or more pages

Looking Back

From the files of Charles Flagg

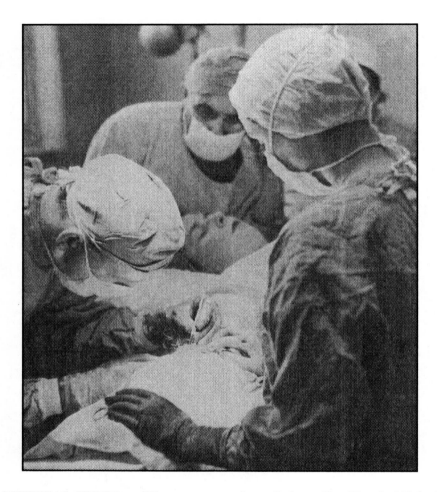

A MEDICAL FIRST — History was made at Quincy City Hospital Feb. 23, 1955, when hypnosis was used as an anesthetic for the first time in Massachusetts. Dr. William P. Ridder performed minor surgery on the arm of Elsie McKinley, 23.

Dr. Naif L. Simon anesthetized the patient with hypnosis during the 25-minute operation. Miss McKinley, a nurse anesthetist at the hospital, returned to her tour of duty directly after the operation.

ORMOND MCGILL
DEAN OF AMERICAN HYPNOTISTS
1913-2005

Through The Years ...

Opinions

"OH NO, I CAN'T GO THROUGH THAT AGAIN!"

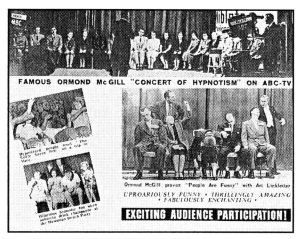

FAMOUS ORMOND McGILL "CONCERT OF HYPNOTISM" ON ABC-TV

Ormond McGill proves "People Are Funny" with Art Linkletter

UPROARIOUSLY FUNNY • THRILLINGLY AMAZING • FABULOUSLY ENCHANTING •

EXCITING AUDIENCE PARTICIPATION!

Ormond McGILL and his SENSATIONAL STAGE PRESENTATION

EAST INDIAN MIRACLES!

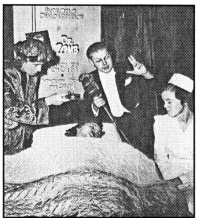

* 31 *

STATE OF NEW HAMPSHIRE

HOUSE OF REPRESENTATIVES

A DECLARATION

*Let it be known that
the New Hampshire House of Representatives,
on this occasion, publicly does recognize
and does grant its hearty and sincere congratulations to*

Ormond McGill

In Recognition Of

his more than 60 years as an author and showman.

*And be it further known that
the New Hampshire House of Representatives,
by virtue of the Speaker's signature inscribed below,
also does duly extend its highest accolades and plaudits.*

Speaker of the House

offered by Representative Dennis H. Fields

The Ormond McGill Chair

ARNOLD FURST
1918-2002

My first exposure to Arnold Furst was during the forties when almost every issue of the popular magazines for magical enthusiasts had write-ups or pictures of this smiling young man as he performed his magic and hypnotism shows for American servicemen throughout the world. Arnold and his globe-trotting magic rabbit were photographers' favorites as they zigzagged to far-off outposts of the South Pacific from 1943 through 1946.

While in Hawaii in 1957 Arnold formed an alliance with Dr. Lester T. Kashiwa to collaborate on the text, *Case Histories in Hypnotherapy*. He received many requests for lecture demonstrations of hypnotism, particularly from medical and dental groups, and this became the reason to start traveling again. During a tour in England, he was awarded an honorary Ph.D. from the Psychiatric Practitioners of London for his contributions to the field of hypnology. While conducting hypnotic demonstrations in Japan, he was asked by Mr. Takeo Omori to teach regular seminars at the Hypnotism and Psychological Institute of Tokyo, which he did, averaging twenty classes a year until 1972. An interesting side note is that many of these demonstrations and seminars were conducted with a translator, since Arnold did not speak Japanese. He also received invitations at this time to conduct courses for physicians and dentists at many U.S. military hospitals and bases in that area.

When asked to explain his approach to the induction of the hypnotic state, Dr. Furst explained, "The patient is not hypnotized because of what is said or how the therapist acts or looks. He responds because a special situation exists and his desire at that particular moment is to please the person who he knows is trying to help him.

"These three conditions must always be present: First—a feeling of rapport. Second—a knowledge that the hypnotist is capable and fully understands what he is doing. Third—there must be strong motivation, a good valid reason for following the instruction.

"All persons who understand simple instructions can be hypnotized. Small children are hypnotized, as are university students, professional people and the aged. Of course, different induction techniques are used for the various levels of intelligence."

Arnold Furst has written many books for magicians, and in the field of hypnotism he is known for his books *Hypnotism for Salesmen, Post Hypnotic Instructions, How to Prepare and Administer Hypnotic Prescriptions*, and *Rapid Induction Hypnosis and Self-Hypnosis*. He has always stressed that hypnosis in itself is neither a cure-all nor a wonder drug, but an effective tool when used by trained therapists. While lecturing at the 106th General Hospital at Kishine Barracks near Tokyo in 1969, he was able to help in the treatment of a soldier suffering with intense pain as a result of almost forty shrapnel wounds. The patient was receiving a maximum dosage of morphine for newer damage but couldn't be evacuated to the States for further treatment until the intensity of the pain subsided.

"He was amazed and happy, too," recalled Arnold, "when I proved to him that he could make the pain go and stay away. His doctor's eyes glisten with tears as he saw his patient's happiness over the prospect of going home."

Arnold was somewhat of a doubting Thomas himself when first exposed to hypnotism many years ago, he explains, when a doctor friend spent until the early morning hours convincing this questioning student "that there is absolutely no danger in placing someone in a hypnotic state and that the therapeutic value of the approach to solving various medical problems is truly immense."

In 1986 he was nominated to join the distinguished Advisory Board of the National Guild of Hypnotists and was awarded the designation of Certified Hypnotherapist, Honoris Causa, in recognition of his contributions to the art, science and philosophy of hypnotism.

In his appearances throughout the world, he found no need to assume the role of the stereotypical stage hypnotist with theatrical gestures and dramatic showmanship. He merely talked to his subjects in a friendly and confident manner, and they comply to his direction within seconds.

JOAN BRANDON
OUTSTANDING FEMME HYPNOTIST OF THE 50S

LIFE

HYPNOSIS
OLD 'BLACK ART' IS NOW ACCEPTED MEDICAL TOOL

ECTS: JEWELS
GLE PARADISE

The BIG Story

A.M.A. VALIDATES USE OF HYPNOSIS

and **LIFE** magazine tells the story ----

Complete article from November 3, 1985
reprinted as a memento of the

1993
National Guild of Hypnotists
Annual Convention and Educational Conference
Nashua, N.H., August 13 - 15, 1993

NOVEMBER 3, 1958 **25** CENTS

OUT OF ANCIENT MAGIC COMES
NEW MEDICAL TOOL

HYPNOSIS

Hypnosis has finally gone medically legitimate. Because it traditionally has been the secret of the stage magician, the public usually has looked on hypnosis as black magic, picturing its practitioners as spell-casting Svengali. But in the past 10 years some 900 U.S. doctors, dentists and psychologists have been quietly employing hypnosis to help their patients. The success has so impressed the American Medical Association that it has now endorsed hypnosis as a therapeutic aid for doctors and dentists properly trained in its use.

This significant vote of confidence means that more Americans soon will be experiencing the feeling of drifting into a vortex of sound—the reassuring, repetitive sound of the hypnotist's voice. They will find that the suggestions his voice plants in their minds can help them through crisises that range from the extreme stress of undergoing open heart surgery without general anesthesia to the problem of gagging at the dentist's. They will discover that hypnosis can put them into a contented, relaxed frame of mind, allay their panic and help them forget their ordeal.

As an anesthetic in surgery, hypnosis persuades the patient he feels no pain, prevents the vomiting, fatigue and loss of appetite that often follows operations. It is specifically useful in operations where general anesthetics should not be used and in childbirth where too much anesthetic can harm the baby. In relieving cancer pain, it is often better than opiates, for it is not habit-forming, does not lose its effect, as narcotics do.

While medical hypnotists are gratified by its new legitimacy, they are afraid hypnosis may stimulate the fad-loving public to clamor for it as everybody's cure-all. This could cause tragic disappointment, for at least one out of 10 patients cannot be hypnotized at all and one out of six will not go into the deep trance needed for painkilling in major surgery. What is more, hypnosis does not cure anything. Compulsive overeating in obese patients, for instance, can be stopped through hypnosis. But this does not remove the cause of the compulsion —the patient may stop eating candy and start chewing his nails.

Research in hypnosis is still so new that its potentials are not fully understood. Startling new findings on the psychiatric uses of hypnosis and its potential threat in psychological warfare will be discussed in future issues of Life. Meanwhile hypnotism's most striking present applications, in the field of childbirth, surgery and therapy, are shown on the following pages.

"Open your eyes, Shirley. Look—look at your baby." At these words, uttered by a Chicago obstetrician, Shirley Mucci came out of a hypnotic trance and saw her minutes-old son. Hypnotized before going into labor, she was conscious of no discomfort during delivery.

Months before, she had shed the anxieties of pregnancy by attending a group clinic for prenatal training where a doctor taught her to hypnotize herself by repeatedly assuring her under hypnosis that she would be able to put herself into a light trance at will when she got home. For 15 minutes each day, Mrs. Mucci had done so, closing her eyes, telling herself she was very relaxed and that her arm was as numb as if it were anesthetized. Then she had said to herself over and over, "I'm completely calm. I am not at all worried."

At the hospital she hypnotized herself again as labor began. Next morning the doctor came by, said, "Ralph will now put his hand on you," said the doctor, "Ralph will reinforce you." In the delivery room the doctor murmured, "Think of yourself doing something very pleasant. Maybe you are gardening ... I want you to pant like a dog. Grunt. Pant." At delivery he said, "You don't feel anything." And Mrs. Mucci did not.

Not all pregnant women can be as fully hypnotized as Mrs. Mucci. Nor should all cases be hypnotized. But for many women the elimination of tension through hypnosis is a blessing. And for those who have to be delivered by Caesarean section yet cannot tolerate required anesthetics, this is an ideal way to have a baby.

For Fred Heywang, five hours of what might have been living hell went by in peace. At Dallas Parkland Memorial Hospital, Psychologist Harold Crasilneck, the hypnotist, kept him relaxed during the awful stress of operation while part of his skull was removed and needlelike instrument inserted deep into his gray matter.

Heywang, who had been suffering from crippling limb tremors for 20 years, had to undergo this without general anesthetic. Surgeon Kemp Clark had to be able to watch his reactions as he penetrated the brain to discover which part was the area controlling spasms and then treat it to stop the spasms. Under hypnosis Heywang was conscious enough for Dr. Clark to see when the tremors stopped. Only once did Heywang sense mild pain, saying, "Oh, brother! It feels like a thousand bites." When he awoke, he recalled little of his trial, raised his arms and gasped, "My palsy's gone."

For Dorothy Haralson, hypnosis meant the end of torture. Her body had been burned when a gas heater exploded in her Irving, Texas home. As healing began, dead tissue had to be cut away, and she was supposed to exercise her badly injured right arm. But even with opiates the pain was so excruciating she refused to move the limb and its muscles contracted.

At Parkland Memorial Hospital her surgeon suggested that Dallas psychologist Harold Crasilneck try hypnosis. Under it she felt nothing during tissue removal. Later he hypnotized her for therapy. "You are getting drowsy," he suggested. "Your eyes are sealed tight, though you are very relaxed. We're going to exercise that arm. Stretch it. When you awake you will continue to move it but this will not be painful." Awakened, she moved her arm. "How do you feel?" asked Dr. Crasilneck. "Just fine," she beamed.

Humbug In The Past, Dangers In Present

The widest use of hypnosis in modern times has been for entertainment, and the medical profession views with considerable alarm the stage magician who puts members of his audience into trances. Both physical and mental harm come from his act. "The use of hypnosis for entertainment purposes." The A.M.A. has flatly stated, "is vigorously condemned." Medical hypnotists hope state governments will pass bills banning hypnosis in the amusement field, but the opposition from entertainers is powerful. In 1957 the city council of Buffalo, N.Y. considered such a resolution. It was opposed by Ring Twelve of the Buffalo Magic Club on grounds of discrimination and was quietly dropped.

Hypnotism has a long history of misuse. Its earlier uses were religious and medical at the same time, for primitive man correlated faith with healing, considering the witch doctor both priest and physician. As far back as the old Stone Age, anthropologists believe, religious leaders awed their caveman audiences by going into hypnotic trances. Ancient soothsayers who gazed into crystals to divine the future undoubtedly fell into trances, believing this gave them foresight. Persian magi and Hindu fakirs practiced self-hypnosis, claiming supernatural healing powers when in this state. The priests of ancient Egypt brought their patients to temples and, using a form of hypnosis, told them the gods would cure them as they slept.

In later centuries certain religions retained self-hypnosis as a spiritual aid. During the 1880s the Christian monks of Mt. Athos in Greece practiced it as part of their devotions. So do Hindu yogis of today. But in medicine hypnosis was not recognized in modern times until the end of the 18th Century. The Franz Anton Mesmer revived and expanded an old and erroneous theory that sickness was due to an imbalance of "universal fluids" which, he believed, could be readjusted by man through a magnetic force. He used a type of hypnotism to control this force and treat patients. Europe's aristocracy took up mesmerism as a fad until a scientific commission, which included Benjamin Franklin, denounced his practices as humbug.

One of Mesmer's disciples, the Marquis de Puysegur, accurately described Mesmer's "magnetism" as artificial somnambulism. The British Surgeon James Braid said it was a state of mind and named it hypnotism. In 1821, in France, the first operation under hypnotic anesthesia was performed. It was followed over the next 60 years by thousands of other operations carried out by European surgeons. Dr. James Esdaile even persuaded the British government to set up three hospitals in Britain and India where hypnosis would be used.

At the turn of the century, hypnosis received a crippling blow. Sigmund Freud tried it to treat hysteria but discarded it as ineffective and turned away from it in favor of psychoanalysis. This nearly ruined hypnotism's reputation. It was not considered valid treatment again until World War I, when it was briefly used to treat "shell shock." But doctors did not understand it and lost interest in it. In World War II the old tool was tried again for combat neuroses. This time doctors began to study its complex nature and to prove its worth.

Today most practicing medical hypnotists are not full-time hypnotists but are doctors who use hypnosis as an aid to their practice. In the U.S. there are about 400 dentists well trained in its use, 250 general practitioners, 150 specialists such as obstetricians, internists, surgeons and anesthesiologist, and 100 psychologists and psychiatrists. Some of these men were recently trained at medical schools but more than half learned techniques by themselves years ago when no good courses were available. Only two U.S. universities now offer extensive training in hypnosis, giving it as a graduate course which is open to any doctor, dentist or psychologist.

Hypnotism's increasing popularity will almost certainly create a shortage of trained practitioners. The first and oldest organization of medical hypnotists in North America today, the Society for Clinical and Experimental Hypnosis, recommends at least a year of training for any doctor or dentist who wants to use hypnosis in his specialty. It fears some doctors will try hypnosis after only a cursory course and, unaware of its limitations, will do more harm than good.

"Quickie courses," warns Dr. Milton V. Kline, editor of the society's journal, "give the men the tool but not the appreciation of how carefully it must be used." He points to the case of a patient who came to him after having been hypnotized by a dentist. With hypnosis the dentist had stopped the man from grinding his teeth. But the man was neurotic and when he could no longer find a teeth-grinding outlet for his tensions, he started to overeat. When Kline got him, his weight had soared from 145 to 288 pounds.

Widespread Application and a Warning

Hypnosis is now being tried in many cases other than major surgery—to treat asthma, hay fever and multiple sclerosis, relieve pain in minor surgery, help patients hold awkward positions for skin grafting and substitute for the needle at the dentist's. But as these applications become more and more varied there is danger that the public will take to hypnosis as heedlessly as it has welcomed tranquilizers. Doctors may be pressured into using it unwisely. To avoid this, Southwestern Medical School in Dallas permits hypnosis only after the case is discussed at a conference of several different specialists.

Dr. Harold Crasilneck advises that hypnosis "should be used only with specific cases that no longer respond to standard treatment." Some doctors may not heed this advice. Having used hypnosis to relieve physical distress during a patient's ulcer operation, for instance, a too ambitious doctor may try to get at the psychosomatic reasons for the ulcer. Unless he is grounded in clinical psychology he can botch this and drive the patient into hysteria.

Unfortunately, healing by untrained hypnotists flourishes in the nation today and the situation may get worse now that hypnosis is medically respectable. Many reputable hypnotists now warn their patient under hypnosis: "You will never under any condition allow yourself to be hypnotized by anyone who is not qualified to do so."

The true nature of hypnosis is still debatable, but in general it acts in the following manner. Usually, for a person to "go under," or be induced into a trance, he must be willing. No one normally can be hypnotized against his will, nor will anyone who is hypnotized perform an act that goes against his best interests. The best subjects are those who want it most—those in great pain.

Induction works only if the person concentrates completely on one repetitive stimulus, somewhat in the way an infant falls asleep to the repeated rocking of his cradle. This stimulus can be sight or sound, or as in the case of the whirling dervish motion. In a typical hypnosis session, the subject responds to only one of his five senses. As he stares fixedly at a small object or a light, his vision becomes fuzzy with fatigue and he is unaware of any sensation except hearing. He pays attention to only one sound, the hypnotist's voice murmuring repetitively, "You are sleepy, so very, very sleepy." The voice gets the brain's undivided attention and literally talks the brain into a sleeplike trance.

As he drifts off, the subject may feel slightly dizzy, as though swaying, floating or falling down a shaft. Objects around him may seem to waver, as if seen under water. His temperature may fall slightly. He may see streaks of light, gaudy kaleidoscopic patterns or complementary colors—a green wall may look yellow. Patients have described such temporary illusions as "I feel as if my body were not here, only my head," or "I am an egg-shaped disk, and you (the doctor) are like a luminous crescent hovering over me."

The illusions and strange feeling of unreality come from the fact that during induction the personality that the patient had when he was awake—his conscious-ness—becomes temporarily altered. With many inhibitions released, he may feel intense emotion—generally elation, but occasionally anger and terror. Then his ability to perceive sensations and to conceive ideas about them change. He will take unreal things for reality, but only if this is suggested to him as an image. For example, one subject had no reaction whatever when informed under hypnosis: "Your temperature is falling." But when told that he was going up into the stratosphere in a plane, the image made him start to shiver and his temperature dropped to 92 degrees.

When a patient is in a trance his subconscious can be influenced. He lacks volition, feels that resistance is too much effort. He is extremely susceptible to suggestion, reacts to what he is told without question or criticism. If he has to undergo surgery, he will, under hypnosis, be convinced that he is pain-free. Physically he will be receiving pain, for damaged nerves will be sending signals to his brain. But psychologically he will not be feeling pain, for his brain will refuse to perceive these signals and coordinate them into the feeling of pain.

How far suggestion, which is intensified in hypnosis, controls the reactions of the human body becomes of increasing importance to doctors as they use hyp-nosis more widely. Recent experiments indicate that hypnosis may affect more than the brain and may actually reduce the nerves' pain signals.

Other tests give startling evidence of hypnotism's power over physical functions, some subjects were given constipating doses of opium under the guise of castor oil; the results were cathartic. A patient whose leg was immobilized with anesthetic was told under hypnosis that he could walk—and he did, as though his leg were normal. Another was advised he was swallowing spoonfuls of honey, and the sugar content of his blood immediately rose and one man, assured he was eating tenderloin, chewed up a blotter with great satisfaction.

LIFE magazine©Time Warner
Reprinted with permission.

The National Guild of Hypnotists, Inc.

Welcome to the National Guild of Hypnotists . . . the world's oldest and largest hypnotism member-organization with over 9,000 active members in 65 countries. We are inclosing information about our organization and the many benefits and resources which are available to you as a valued member.

The *Journal of Hypnotism* is the most widely-read magazine of its type and is mailed to our active members in December, March, June, and September. The *Hypno-Gram* is more of a tabloid style publication and is mailed for Jan/Feb, Apr/May, July/Aug and Oct/Nov. Both of these publications also contain information about Guild activities such as continuing education workshops and the annual convention.

Our NGH annual convention and educational conference has become reknown as "the largest and friendliest hypnotism convention", and is held each year in August in New England. Our most recent convention had an adjunct faculty of 190 presenters with 145 one hour seminars, 102 two hour workshops, 18 three hour workshops and 29 pre and post convention workshops. It is the year's single most important event exclusively for hypnotists and hypnotherapists. Continuing-education credits are given to attendees of the convention

Each February we hold our annual Solid Gold weekend conference in Las Vegas or California. This is a smaller two-day conference with 10 to 12 presenters, and continuing-education credits are also awarded for attendance.

An outstanding resource is our Video Rental Library which is available only to NGH members. Many of the convention seminars and workshops, which were recorded live, are available for rental and a catalog is enclosed with this letter. Audio tapes of all workshops and seminars are also available for purchase. We can provide the VHS versions in PAL when necessary and currently are re-mastering to also have CD and DVD versions available soon.

NATIONAL GUILD OF HYPNOTISTS CHRONOLOGY

1950–51 • National Guild of Hypnotists formed Sept. 1950—George Rogers officially named chairman in Spring of 1951. *Note:* Charter members still living and active in Guild at publication 2006; Dr. Dwight Damon, Dr. John C. Hughes, Arnold Levinson and Maurice Kershaw.

1951 • Annual dues are $3 to cover membership card and certificate as chapters are formed across the U.S.

1951 • *Journal of Hypnotism*—1st edition full magazine format published in May —Dr. Rexford L.North, editor/publisher; contributing editors: Harry Arons, Dwight Damon, Bernard Yanover.

1953 • 1st *Journal of Hypnotism* color cover featured Ormond McGill.

1956 • Changed name and format of *Journal of Hypnotism* to *Hypnotism* (tabloid newspaper format).

1956–1986 • Charter members of the NGH met informally and actively promoted the profession of hypnotism through educational programs run throughout the world. Charter members Dwight Damon and John Hughes also presented basic courses and educational workshops throughout the Midwest and New England while pursuing their doctoral studies. Members who met throughout this 30 year period decided to establish the NGH as the leading national society of hypnosis in the US using the facilities and expertise of Elsom Eldridge's Achievement Center facilities and computer expert David Hubbell.

1986 • Annual dues for a certified member are $55 and include membership card, re-designed certificate and the start of member benefits.

1959 • International Hypnological Association founded in 1953 merged with NGH.

1986 • First hardcover text published by NGH was *Power Hypnosis* by Drs. Damon and Hughes.

1986 • Certification and Advanced training classes presented across the U.S. by Damon, Hughes, LaVelle, and Bien.

1986 • Dr. John Hughes formed the Philippine Hypnodontic Society while teaching health professionals in that country.

1986 • Boston and NYC chapters re-activated and Newark, NJ chapter formed.

1986 • The *New Journal of Hypnotism* launched in March.

1986 • Minimum number of certification training hours established as 25 hours.

1986 • RHy (Registered Hypnotherapist) designation first instituted.

1987 • The *Hypno-Gram* launched in January as a 4-page newsletter (Currently 24-pages with columnists and guest articles) Regular columnists: Dr. Dwight Damon, Charles Francis, Dave Crosby. Robert Otto, and Don Rice.

1987 • First East Coast workshop presented with Arnold Furst, PhD.

1987 • First East Coast workshop presented with Ormond McGill, "Dean of American Hypnotists".

1988 • Name change of *The New Journal of Hypnotism* back to the original title of *The Journal of Hypnotism*.

1988 • Minimum number of training hours raised to one college semesters (50 hours) + 25 hours independent study for certification.

1988 • First East Coast workshop presented with Gil Boyne.

1988 • Elsom Eldridge appointed Convention Director.

1988 • 1st annual convention held in Danvers, Mass with 250 attendees. Educator of the Year Awards—1st recipients:
    Ormond McGill and Charles Tebbetts.
Journalism Award—1st recipient Dr. John C. Hughes.
President's Award—1st recipient George Bien.
NGH Scholarship Award—1st recipient Katherine Dewar.

1988 • Audio cassette workshop/seminar archives established.

1989 • NGH helps charter and contributes seed money to Council of Professional Hypnosis Organizations (COPHO).

1989 • Lydia Hubbell appointed Convention Facilities Coordinator.

1989 • 2nd annual convention held in NYC with 500 attendees.

1989 • Aug. 18 proclaimed National Guild of Hypnotists Day in New York City by Mayor David Dinkins.

1990 • 750 attendees as the NGH convention moved to NH for the next 15 years becoming "The Largest and Friendliest Hypnotism Convention"

New Awards which were authorized through the years:

Dr. Rexford L. North Memorial Award — 1st recipient: Steven A. LaVelle.

Member of the Year — 1st recipient: Ed Hightower.

Humanities Award & Grant — Penny Dutton Raffa.

Ormond McGill Chair established 1992 — 1st recipient: Marx Howell Awarded by convention attendees peer voting.

Charles Tebbetts Award 1993 — 1st recipient: George Bien.

Certified Instructor of the Year 1992 — 1st recipient: Ed Morris.

William N. Curtis Religion & Hypnotism Award 1998
By the Clergy Hypnotists special interest group.
    Awarded by convention attendees peer voting:
Hypnotism Humanities — 1st recipient: Michael Ellner.
Hypnosis Research — 1st recipients: Connie Palinsky & Virginia Baxter.
Meritorious Service — 1st recipient: Charles Tebbetts.
International Hypnosis Service Award — 1st recipient: Dr. Rufino N. Achacosa.
Hypnosis Video — 1st recipient: Rex Trailer.
TV Journalism — 1st recipient: Anna Vitale.

1990 • First professional hypnotism organization to require continuing education credits of 15 hours for active certification status.

1991 • Train The Trainers program and core-curriculum launched with Dr. Richard Harte as Training Director.

1991 • Introduced professionally-written ads, columns, and brochures for NGH members.

1991 • Minimum number of training hours established as one college semesters (50 hours) for certification.

1992 • Member Video Library established as another first for any hypnotism organization.

1992 • NGH continuing-education workshop program for NGH members developed and initiated by Don Mottin.

1993 • NGH incorporated as NH non-profit corporation "to encourage educational programs to further the knowledge and understanding of hypnotism and to provide continuing-education programs in hypnosis and related topics" and to assure future continuation of the Guild.

1993 • Effort begun to amend Illinois Clinical Psychologist License Act which had been transformed into a practice protection act restricting the practice of hypnotism to licensed health care professionals. Launched first round of corrective legislation that failed by a single vote.

1993 • NGH honored by the 103rd Congress of the United States with a tribute published in the Congressional *Record*.

1993 • Member Ed Morris asked to participate in IBS/Hypnosis research at Dartmouth's Hitchcock Medical Center.

1993 • Legislative kits developed and distributed NGH chapters and state committees.

1993 • Hypnosis Educational Council International founded in 1980 merged with NGH.

1993 • Professional Liability insurance becomes available to all NGH members from an A++ rated company.

1993 • NGH Gold Visa Card made available for our members thru MBNA.

1994 • National Federation of Hypnotists local 104 is chartered by OPEIU, AFL/CIO, CLC NFH 104 union activities include: Legislative action in:
- California, Florida, Tennessee, Illinois, Indiana, Iowa, Louisiana, Massachusetts, Missouri, Nebraska, New Hampshire, New Jersey, New York,Texas, Utah,Vermont, Washington.

- Represented our profession at Union Trade Shows in: Detroit, Las Vegas, New Orleans, a National Health-Care Conference in Washington, DC, and OPEIU, AFL/CIO/CLC Conferences in: Chicago and Fort Lauderdale.

1994 • C. Scot Giles appointed Legislative Liaison Officer for NGH/NFH .

1994 • New Jersey Hypnocounselor Law enacted thru the efforts of members Tony DeMarco and John Gatto with assistance of NFH, OPEIU/AFL.

1994 • NGH donated 1993 convention show proceeds plus VISA royalties to COPHO for Legislative Fund.

1994 • NGH Ethics Committee appointed and protocol developed.

1995 • CH (Certified Hypnotherapist) designation replaces RHy (Registered Hypnotherapist).

1995 • "The Year of McGill" as NGH honored Ormond McGill, "Dean of American Hypnotists."

1995 • Meetings re: Registration Bills in Massachusetts and New Hampshire.

1995 • Annual NGH convention hits the national wire services and also gets a mention on TV in Jay Leno's monologue.

1996 • National Board of Hypnosis Education/Certification founded 1989 merged with NGH.

1996 • NH, ME and VT Registration Bills introduced with union assistance.

1998 • New Hampshire—Introduced Registration Bill in NH with union assistance.

1996 • Renewal of Florida Hypnotist Exemption in Mental Health and Psychology License laws passed.The bill renewing the exemption was the final bill passed on the last day of the legislative session, after intense union and NGH lobbying.

1997 • National Association of Clergy Hypnotherapists founded in 1983 merged with NGH.

1997 • NGH produced and distributed the "Extend Your Horizons" video.

1997 • Member Video Rental Library adds PAL equipment to accommodate members in other countries.

1997 • Illinois—Passed PA 90-473 which amended the Psychologist License Act to permit hypnotism to be practiced by unlicensed persons. This bill was passed after four legislative attempts.

1997 • California—Defeated attempted legislation restricting the practice of hypnotism unfairly in a way that benefited only certain organizations.

1998 • NGH produced and distributed the "Women and Hypnosis" video.

1998 • Jereme Bachand appointed as Web Master and Communications Director.

1998 • NGH Certification Board created to improve professionalism of practitioners.

1998 • NGH website (ngh.net) established on the Internet.

1998 • Minimum number of certification training hours raised to two college semesters (100 hours).

1998 • Legislation to protect the right of professional hypnotists to practice introduced experimentally in MA, VT, NH and ME.

1998 • The Honorable James Edgar, Governor of Illinois, congratulates hypnotists on protecting their right to practice.

1998 • Exemption for hypnotists inserted in pending restrictive psychology legislation in Iowa.

1998 • State of Mississippi agrees with NGH not to consider hypnotism a regulated psychological practice.

1998 • NGH picks up pieces of failed legislative efforts by other organizations in Tennessee and Georgia and organizes its own legislative teams in those states.

1998 • State of Nebraska agrees not to consider hypnotism a regulated psychological practice.

1999 • NGH Certification course accepted at Medgar Evers College— City University of New York with Certified Instructor Ed Hightower.

1999 • *Hypnosis Today*—our magazine for consumers was launched.

1999 • NGH Board Certification examines an initial group of candidates.

1999 • Blocked hostile legislation in New York that would have restricted the practice of hypnotism to licensed professionals.

1999 • Killed reintroduced legislation in Iowa that would have restricted hypnotism to licensed professionals.

1999 • Indiana—Intervened to halt abuse by the state Hypnotist Committee which oversees the certification of hypnotists. Eventually we would file and win two lawsuits against the Committee, one filed jointly with the American Civil Liberties Union. These legal victories resulted in a restructuring of the Committee with several members replaced and rules rewritten.

1999 • Illinois—Filed an experimental license law for hypnotists which passed the Senate before being blocked in the House by the medical society.

1999 • Georgia—NGH legislative team blocks a restrictive license law for counselors that would have limited the practice of hypnotism to only state licensed professionals.

1999 • Produced a video instruction kit to help NGH Chapters do legislative and lobbying work.

1999–2000 • Received Federal trademark authorization of National Guild of Hypnotists, *Journal of Hypnotism, Hypno-Gram and Hypnosis Today.*

1990–2004 • National Guild of Hypnotists Week proclamations by successive governors of New Hampshire.

1990–2004 • Declarations and Resolutions by New Hampshire Senate and House of Representatives.

2000 • NGH core curriculum has been translated into: Chinese, Danish, Dutch, French, and Polish

2000 • CEU Quiz for members inaugurated in the December issue of the *Journal of Hypnotism*.

2000 • Recognition from the United Kingdom Confederation of Hypnotherapy Organizations.

2000 • Iowa—Once again defeated a restrictive regulatory law (HB285) that would have prevented hypnotists from practicing.

2000 • Georgia—Defeated a restrictive counselor license law (HB271) that would have limited the practice of hypnotism to persons licensed under that law.

2000 • Kentucky—Defeated a restrictive hypnotism certification law (SB 283) that would have allowed only graduates of specific schools to practice 2000 Illinois—met with the Illinois Medical Association to explore ways hypnotists and physicians could work cooperatively.

2001 • Client Bill of Rights (CBOR) developed and presented for member use.

2001 • "Hypnotic Outcomes" column established in the *Journal of Hypnotism*.

2001 • *Journal of Hypnotism* color covers inaugurated with June issue.

2001 • Hypnosis Information Network founded in 1990 merged with NGH.

2001 • NGH Code of Ethics updated.

2001 • NGH Standards of Practice established.

2001 • Georgia—Arranged veto of a restrictive law (SB 119) that would have limited the practice of hypnotism to persons licensed to practice mental health care.

2001 • Illinois—Introduced a bill (SB 79) that would require all hypnotists to practice in accordance with NGH Standards of Practice.

2001 • Louisiana—Defeated a license law for hypnotists that would have allowed the local Chapter of the NGH to appoint the regulatory body. It is the policy of the NGH to oppose all self-serving legislation, even if beneficial to the NGH at the expense of other organizations.

2001 • New York—Defeated a restrictive license law (AB 9214) that would have limited the practice of hypnotism to physicians, psychologists, counselors and social workers.

2001 • Ohio—Negotiated with the Psychology Board for an understanding that hypnotists practicing within NGH Standards of Practice would not be considered to be in violation of that state's Psychology License Law.

2001 • Rhode Island—Supported a Complementary and Alternative Medicine Freedom of Access Law.

2002 • Professional Terminology established.

2002 • NGH member Internet Hotline established.

2002 • Melody Bachand appointed Executive Director.

2002 • NGH Bookstore went on-line.

2002 • Email bulletins, scripts, and legislative alerts e-mailed to members on a regular basis.

2002 • Texas—Retained local lobbyists and assembled a legislative committee that was successful in blocking enforcement of Cease and Desist Orders that had been distributed to some hypnotists in that state.

2002 • Florida—Obtained an Attorney General ruling that hypnotists who practiced within NGH Standards did not violate Florida Law, and used that ruling to issue a Cease and Desist Order to the State of Florida demanding it not enforce Cease and Desist Orders it and issued to some hypnotists.The government agreed.

2002 • Florida—Negotiated with the Psychology Board to clarify the nature of our exemption.

2002 • Florida—Began financial support of a group seeking to pass a Complementary and Alternative Medicine Freedom of Access Law.

2002 • California—Financially supported passage of a Complementary and Alternative Medicine Freedom of Access Law.

2003 • Great Britain—Shaun Brookhouse was appointed NGH International Affairs Officer.

2003 • NGH CEU courses inaugurated in other countries with Maurice Kershaw teaching Pediatric Hypnosis in London.

2003 • Hypnosisdomains.com—Another member benefit was inaugurated.

2003 • Iowa—Gave seed money for a local committee to seek a Complementary & Alternative Medicine Freedom of Access Law.

2003 • Georgia—Gave financial support of effort to pass Complementary and Alternative Medicine Freedom of Access Law in that state.

2003 • Indiana—Blocked a proposed change in legislation that would have restricted hypnotism to physicians, counselors, psychologists and social workers and banned further credentialing of hypnotists.

2003 • New York—Began work to control the interpretation of provisions of a recently-passed mental health license law.

1991–2004 • NGH Certification programs that have been developed are:

1991 • Forensic Hypnosis—developed by George Baranowski, CI, FNGH.

1998 • Pediatric Hypnotism—developed by Don Mottin, CI, FNGH.

1999 • Emergency Hypnotism—developed by by Don Mottin, CI, FNGH.

1999 • Complementary Medical Hypnotism—developed by Rev. C. Scot Giles, CI, FNGH.

2003 • Sports Hypnotism—developed by Bob Reese, CH.

2003 • Clinical Hypnotism (13 month curriculum) developed by Don Mottin, CI, FNGH.

2004 • Hypno-Coaching developed by Lisa Halpin, CI, BCH.

Publications that have merged with NGH pubs are: *Hypnotism* (est.1956–merged 1986), *Hypnotic Education Bulletin,* (est.1942–merged 1990), *HEC International Newsletter* (est.1963–merged 1990), *DEEPENING* (est.1983–merged 1997),

1986–2004 • Partial list of media which featured NGH:

Readers Digest Family Guide to Natural Medicine—Grolier Book of Knowledge; *Bottom Line Personal; Business Week Consumer Reports*; *Redbook; Women's Week; Woman's Health; Newsweek; Astra Opua* (Greece); *NY Times*

PBS TV; TV's 20/20; Dateline shows; British Royal Free & University College Medical School CD-ROM

2004 • nghinfo.com (for public information and referrals) is established on the Internet.

2004 • Annual dues for a certified member are $95 and now include multiple benefits. Currently 7225 active members in 45 countries.

2004 • Train The Trainers programs are now being conducted outside the US.

2004 • There are currently 59 NGH chapters in the U.S. and 18 in other countries.

2004 • NGH certification courses are being taught in countries around the world by over 450 Certified Instructors.

2004 • Accreditation credentials approved from Britain's NCFE for Clinical graduates and Certified Instructors.

2004 • National P.R. program has reached a readership of 1,426,652 in the past six months.

2004 • Hawaii—Defeated a bill (HCR 22) that would have restricted the practice of hypnotism to psychologists, physicians, social workers and counselors.

2004 • Minnesota—Negotiating protective legislation (Ch 146a) to protect the right of hypnotists to practice after the repeal of the Unlicensed Mental Health Provider laws.

2004 • New York—Negotiating an agreement that hypnotists practicing within NGH Standards and Terminology would not be deemed in violation of a new license law for counselors.

2004 • Texas—Reorganizing a legislative team to prepare to launch exemption legislation in the next session of the legislature.

2004 • Pennsylvania's Harcum College approves NGH core-curriculum for college credits with future on-campus classes being planned.

2004 • Internet and CD-ROM archival program development in planning stages.

2004 • Six important new books are under development for the profession and consumers.

2005 • January 4th officially becomes known and promoted as "World Hypnotism Day." Website is: Worldhypnotismday.com.

2005 • October 19th: 92-year-old Ormond McGill, Dean of American Hypnotists, "passes onward."

About the Author . . .

Dwight F. Damon, D.C., CI, FNGH, was born in Nashua, NH, in 1932. He was educated in the Nashua school system, Phillips Exeter Academy, Cushing Academy (graduated 1949), Emerson College, and Palmer College of Chiropractic (graduated 1959).

Dr. Damon served three years in the USCG and was discharged in 1954 as RM2. He is a member of Phi Alpha Tau, the Masons, the Shriners, the Elks, the New England Showmen's Association, the Showfolks of Sarasota, the International Brotherhood of Magicians, the Academy of Magical Arts, and other professional and fraternal organizations. The author of three textbooks on magic and balloon sculpturing, he was founder of Success Seekers clubs and Ideas For Success Seminars; a writer and teacher in the field of human potential and motivation, associate editor of *The Journal of Hypnotism* (1950–52), a writer and teacher in the field of hypnotism; co-author of *Power Hypnosis* with Dr. John C. Hughes; a student of and assistant to Dr. Rexford L. North at the Hypnotism Center in Boston, MA; and president of the National Guild of Hypnotists, Inc., 1986 to the present time; and editor of the *Journal of Hypnotism*™ and *Hypno-Gram*™.

Dr. Damon has had a lengthy career in show business and was cited as "New England's Youngest Professional Magician" in *Who's Who In Entertainment* in 1945. He appeared as a regular featured entertainer on WOC-TV in Davenport, Iowa from 1956–1959, and produced and starred in his own weekly live children's show on WMUR-TV in Manchester, New Hampshire, for seventeen years, starting in 1960.

He maintained a professional practice as a Doctor of Chiropractic and a Hypnotherapist in Merrimack, New Hampshire for thirty-five years before deciding to devote full-time to building the National Guild of Hypnotists as the largest and oldest organization of its kind and establishing recognition for the profession of hypnotism/hypnotherapy. As a 1951 founding member of the NGH, he has never wavered in his "Big Idea" for NGH members and professional hypnotists around the world, and has seen much of it become a reality. Dr. Damon has spoken before and been honored by many other professional hypnotism groups for his efforts.

Former New Hampshire governor Meldrim Thomson appointed Dwight Damon as "N.H.'s Magical Goodwill Ambassador." He has also received many citations in recognition of his work with the Jerry Lewis Telethon, Crotched Mt. Children's Hospital, Kennedy Memorial Hospital. Dr. Damon was named "Citizen of the Year" by the Merrimack Chamber of Commerce in 1978 and also by the Merrimack Kiwanis in 1987. In 2005 the *NH Union Leader* dubbed him "The Face of Deerfield Fair" for his forty-four years at the fair and twenty-four years as the fair's Entertainment Superintendent.

As president of the National Guild of Hypnotists, Inc. and the National Federation of Hypnotists, 104, OPEIU, AFL/CIO, Dr. Damon is proud to be able to bring his recollections of the early days of the Guild and the story of the amazing stone-deaf hypnotist, Dr. Rexford L. North, to the present generation of hypnotists, hypnologists, and reading public.

Grateful acknowledgement is made to Dr. John C. Hughes, Maurice Kershaw, Dr. Arnold Levison, Larry Garrett and others for contributions of photos and artifacts. A special thank you to Melody Damon Bachand, BCH, NGH Executive Director, for her patience and diligence in getting it all together.

Hypnoclassics@aol.com

Contact Info For: Dr. Dwight F. Damon, President
National Guild of Hypnotists, Inc.
P.O. Box 308
Merrimack, NH 03054-0308
(603) 429-9438
Docvox@ngh.net

Hypnoclassics
P.O. Box 1738
Merrimack, NH 03054-1738
Hypnoclassics@aol.com

National Guild of Hypnotists, Inc.
P.O. Box 308
Merrimack, NH 03054-0308
(603) 429-9438
ngh@ngh.net
www.ngh.net

Printed in the United States
54987LVS00006B/1-306

9 781885 846099